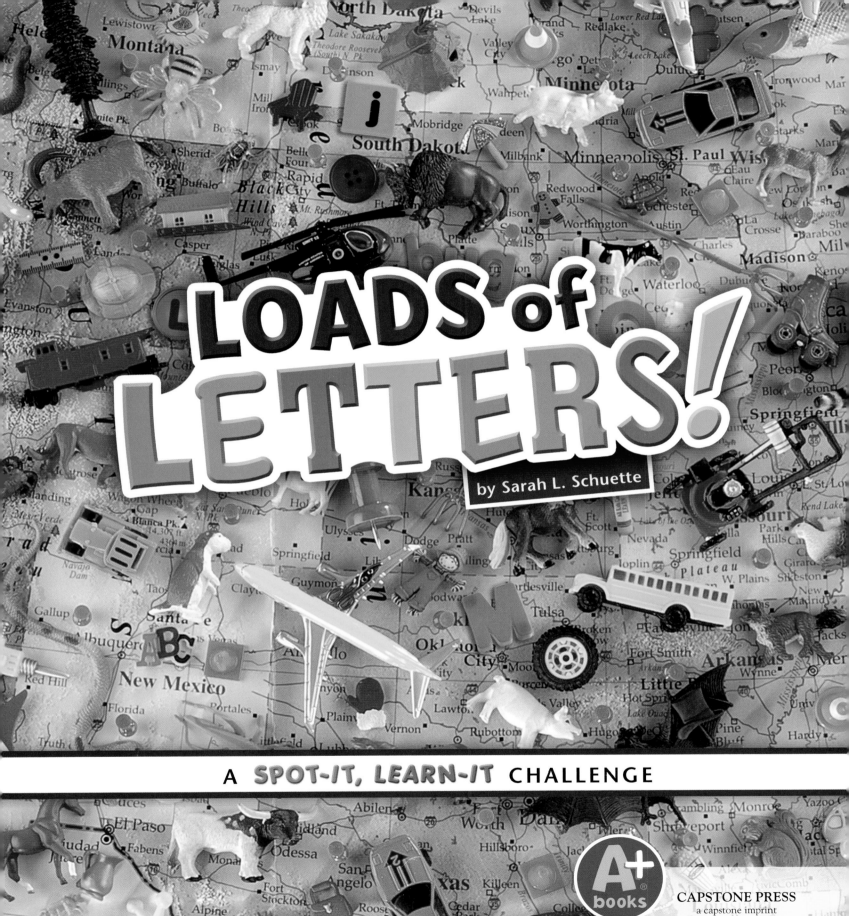

LOADS of LETTERS!

by Sarah L. Schuette

A SPOT-IT, LEARN-IT CHALLENGE

A+ books

CAPSTONE PRESS
a capstone imprint

A+ Books are published by Capstone Press,
1710 Roe Crest Drive, North Mankato, Minnesota 56003
www.capstonepub.com

Library of Congress Cataloging-in-Publication Data
Cataloging-in-publication information is on file with the Library of Congress.
ISBN 978-1-4765-5111-1 (board book)
ISBN 978-1-4765-5948-3 (eBook PDF)
ISBN 978-1-4765-4013-9 (library binding)
ISBN 978-1-4765-5103-6 (paperback)

Editorial Credits
Jeni Wittrock, editor; Juliette Peters, designer; Wanda Winch, media researcher;
Eric Manske, production specialist; Sarah Schuette, photo stylist; Marcy Morin,
photo scheduler

The author dedicates this book to her Goddaughter Muriel Hilgers.

Photo Credits
all photos by Capstone Studio/Karon Dubke

Note to Parents, Teachers, and Librarians
Spot It, Learn It is an interactive series that supports literacy development and reading
enjoyment. Readers utilize visual discrimination skills to find objects among fun-to-
peruse photographs with busy backgrounds. Readers also build vocabulary through
thematic groupings, develop visual memory ability through repeated readings, and
improve strategic and associative thinking skills by experimenting with different
visual search methods.

Printed in the United States of America in Stevens Point, Wisconsin.
092013   00007773WZS14

Table of Contents

Alphabet

Can you find the word **team**?

Find a **green R**.

Can you find a **blue O**?

Spell the word **math** with the letters you find.

Find the things that start with **L**.

Find a **yellow B**.

How many **Q**s can you find?

a is for _____
b is for _____
c is for _____
d is for _____
e is for _____
f is for _____

Seeds

Find the word **melon**.

How many times can you find the word **pumpkin**?

Can you see a **welcome** sign?

Spot the word **good**.

How many things begin with the letter **C**?

Can you spell **cat** with **brown letters**?

ONION

LETTUCE

SWEET CORN

BASIL

OKRA

PEAS

CUCUMBER

LIMA BEAN

BRUSSEL SPROUTS

RHUBARB

RUTA

BLOOM 10¢

Breakfast

Can you see two letter **X**s?

How many letter **K**s
can you find?

Spot four lowercase **a**'s.

Now find the lowercase **i**'s.

Look for the word **cookies**.

Spell **kite** with the letters
you find.

Trains

Find a **white T**.

How many times do you see the word **northern**?

Can you see two **J**s?

Spell the word **cage** with the letters you find.

Look for all of the letter **G**s.

Spot the word **police**.

ONE WAY

638

POLICE

CHATTANOOGA

EMERGENCY

B E O T

We can
handle it.

BURLINGTON
NORTHERN

BN
100 024

Be Specific—
ship UNION PACIFIC

j

689

11

Games

Can you find the wooden **A**, **B**, and **C** letters?

See if you can spot the word **one**.

Where is a **black S**?

Search for things that start with **T**.

Find a **white N**.

Can you spell the word **soap**?

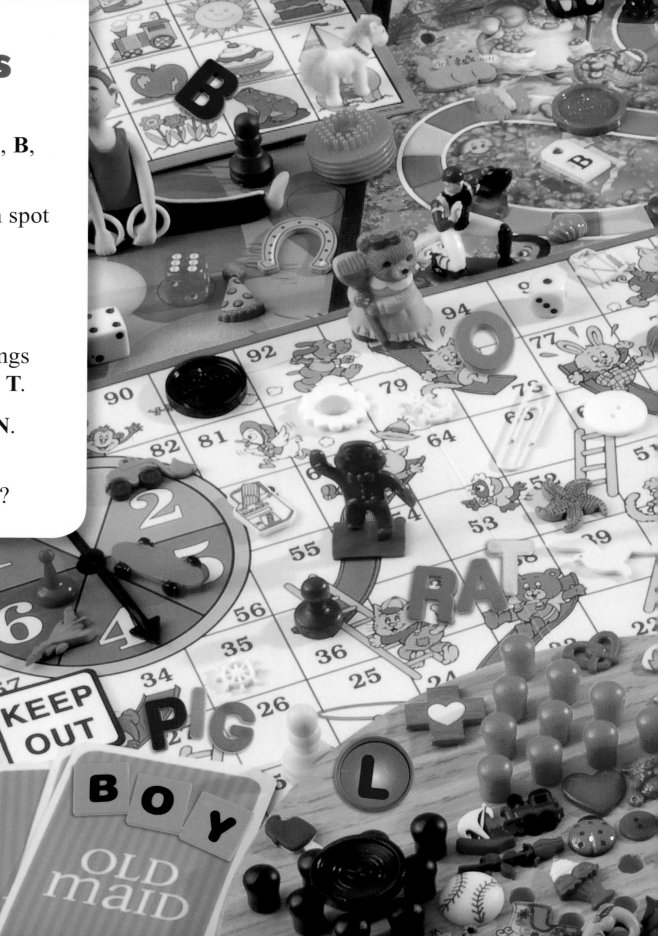

ONE WAY

TEAM

97
75
74
68
50
40
20
31
10

C

13

Homework

How many times can you spot the word **rug**?

Can you see a **pink E**?

Search for the word **place**.

Where is a **pink Z**?

Find the word **you**.

Look for things that start with the letter **F**.

States

Find the word **bug**.

Do you see a **blue O**?

How many letter **Ls** do you see?

How many things start with letter **B**?

See if you can spot the word **wagon**.

Can you spell **mug**?

Toys

How many **Ms** can you see?

Spot the word **racer**.

Do you see the word **card**?

How many times can you find a letter **Y**?

Spell **top** with the letters you find.

Where is a yellow **R**?

Lunch

Can you find the word **learn**?

Can you spot the name **Sarah**?

Try to find a **yellow K**.

Where is the word **fan**?

Can you see a **white C**?

Look for objects that begin with a letter **F**.

Movies

Look for the word **box**.

How many things start with the letter **I**?

Try to find the word **salt**.

How many **V**s can you see?

How many things start with a letter **E**?

Spot the word **boom**.

Puzzle

Spell **play** with the **white letter beads**.

Can you see the word **notes**?

Find a **purple A**.

Look for things that begin with **P**.

How many **Ls** do you see?

Can you find a **purple E** bead?

25

Scrapbook

Find the word **rabbit**.

Where is an **orange D**?

Spell **yellow** with the **silver letters**.

Can you spot a **brown Q**?

Look for a **green X**.

Do you see 2 **silver Y**s?

Spot Even More

Alphabet • page 4

How many objects begin with the letter **P**? Find the word **popcorn**. Spell **log** with **wooden letters**.

Seeds • page 6

How many **brown letter A**s can you find? Spell **soil** with **brown letters**. Try to spot a **green u**.

Breakfast • page 8

Can you spell **Saturday** with **letters on green blocks**? Find the word **crayon**. How many things start with the letter **O**?

Trains • page 10

How many things start with the letter **T**? Find the word **new** twice. Spell **Tango** with the **white letters**.

Games • page 12

Can you see the word **space**? How many **red things** begin with the letter **R**? Look for the word **checkers**.

Homework • page 14

How many things start with the letter **w**? Can you spell **goat** with letters you find? Try to spot a **red C**.

States • page 16

Can you find the word **truth**? Look for all the things that start with **U**. How many times do you see the word **Palm**?

Toys • page 18

This time find the word **bell**. Look for the objects that begin with letter **P**. See if you can spot **three red L**s.

Lunch • page 20

Next find the word **chalk**. Look for an object that begins with the letter **X**. Look for the **green O**.

Movies • page 22

Spot the word **cola**. Try to find objects that begin with the letter **V**. How many objects begin with **I**?

Puzzle • page 24

How many things begin with the letter **Z**? Now find things that begin with **G**. Spell **queen** with small **black letters**.

Scrapbook • page 26

Which **letters** look like the **gray horseshoe**? Can you find a **pale red C**? Spot the word **Cereal**. Search for a **yellow A**.

Extreme Challenge

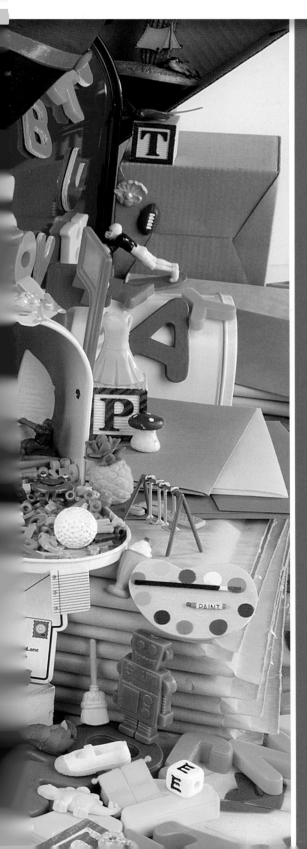

Just can't get enough Spot-It action? Here's an extra letters challenge.

How many times can you find the word **mail**?

Find the **red letter B**s.

Do you see the word **splash**?

Can you find the letters to spell **sun**?

Spot the word **soap**.

Try to find the word **zoo**.

Can you see the **red V**?

Next find the **blue a**.

Search for the word **soup**.

Look for the word **learn**.

Find the word **sunshine**.

Can you spell **newspaper** with the letters you see?

Read More

Boldt, Mike. *123 Versus ABC.* New York: Harper, 2013.

Ghigna, Charles. *The Alphabet Parade.* My Little School House. North Mankato, Minn.: Picture Window Books, 2013.

Thomas, Isabel. *Alphabet Fun: Making Letters with Your Body.* Chicago: Heinemann Library, 2014.

Internet Sites

FactHound offers a safe, fun way to find Internet sites related to this book. All of the sites on FactHound have been researched by our staff.

Here's all you do:

Visit *www.facthound.com*

Type in this code: 9781476540139

Super-cool stuff! Check out projects, games and lots more at www.capstonekids.com